ICH SCHLAFE GERN IN MEINEM EIGENEN BETT
I LOVE TO SLEEP IN MY OWN BED

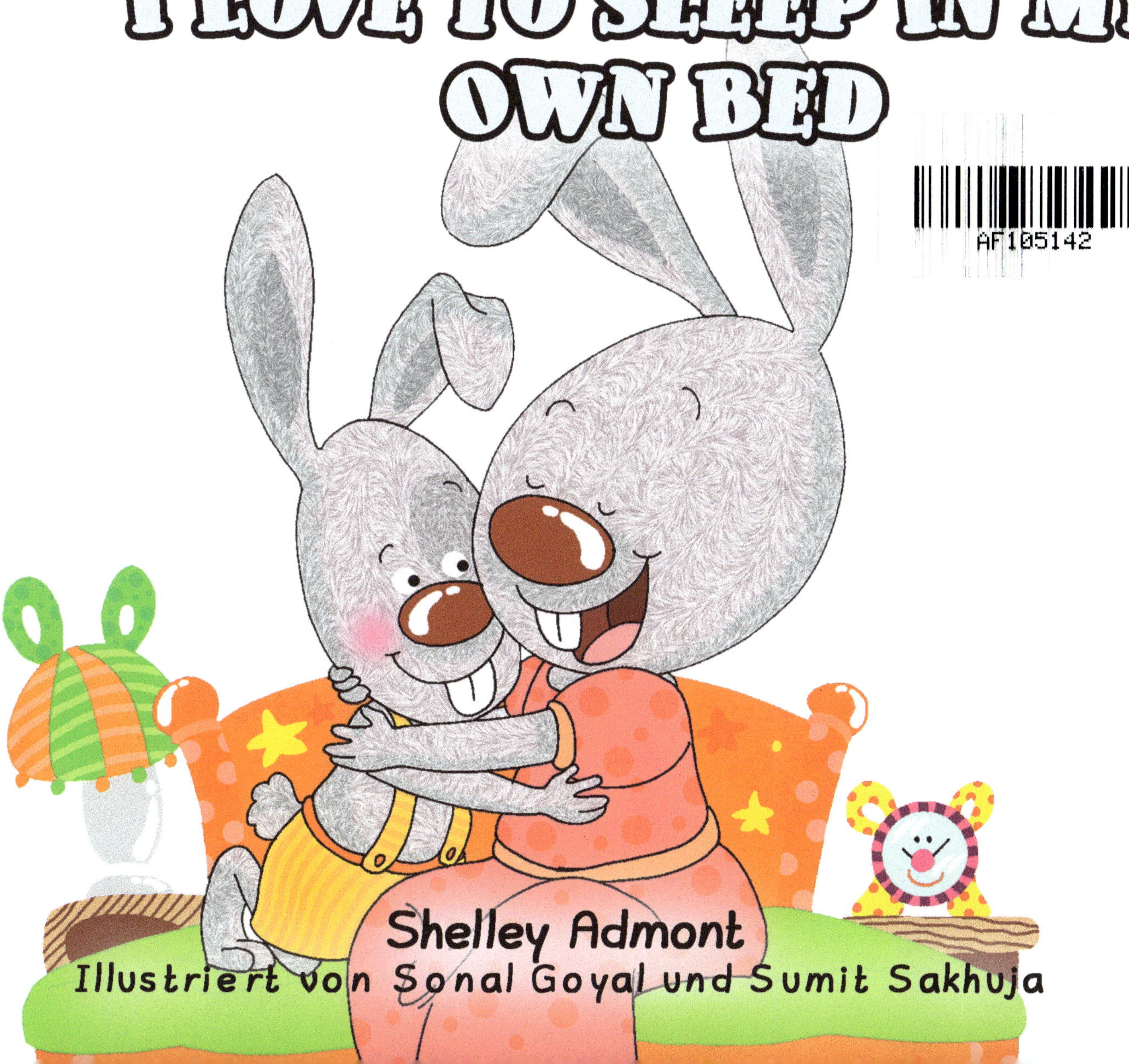

Shelley Admont
Illustriert von Sonal Goyal und Sumit Sakhuja

www.kidkiddos.com
Copyright©2013 by S. A. Publishing ©2017 by KidKiddos Books Ltd.
support@kidkiddos.com

All rights reserved. No part of this book may be reproduced in any form or by any electronic or mechanical means, including information storage and retrieval systems, without written permission from the publisher or author, except in the case of a reviewer, who may quote brief passages embodied in critical articles or in a review.

Alle Rechte vorbehalten. Kein Teil dieses Buches darf in irgendeiner Form oder durch irgendwelche elektronischen oder mechanischen Mitteln, einschließlich Informationen Regalbediengeräte schriftlich beim Verlag, mit Ausnahme von einem Rezensenten, kurze Passagen in einer Bewertung zitieren darf reproduziert, ohne Erlaubnis.

Second edition, 2019

Translated from English by Tess Parthum
Aus dem Englischen übersetzt von Tess Parthum

Library and Archives Canada Cataloguing in Publication data
I love to sleep in my own bed (German English Bilingual Edition)/ Shelley Admont
ISBN: 978-1-5259-1894-0 paperback
ISBN: 978-1-77268-624-1 hardcover
ISBN: 978-1-77268-213-7 ebook

Please note that the German and English versions of the story have been written to be as close as possible. However, in some cases they differ in order to accommodate nuances and fluidity of each language.

Für die, die ich am meisten liebe–S.A.

For those I love the most–S. A.

Jimmy, der kleine Hase, lebte mit seiner Familie im Wald. Er wohnte in einem wunderschönen Haus mit seiner Mama, seinem Papa und zwei älteren Brüdern.

Jimmy, a little bunny, lived with his family in the forest. He lived in a beautiful house with his mom, dad, and two older brothers.

Jimmy schlief nicht gern in seinem eigenen Bett.

Jimmy didn't like to sleep in his own bed.

Eines Abends vor dem Schlafengehen fragte er seine Mama: „Mama, darf ich mit dir in deinem Bett schlafen? Ich schlafe wirklich gar nicht gern allein in meinem Bett."

One night, before going to bed, he asked his mom, "Mom, can I sleep in your bed with you? I really don't like sleeping in my bed alone."

„Lass es uns so machen. Du gehst in dein Bett und ich nehme dich in den Arm, decke dich zu und lese dir und deinen Brüdern eine Geschichte vor."

"Let's do this. You get into your bed, and I'll hug you, tuck you in, and read you and your brothers a story."

„Und dann gebe ich dir einen Kuss und bleibe bei dir sitzen bis du eingeschlafen bist."

"Then, I'll give you a kiss and sit with you until you fall asleep."

„Na gut", willigte Jimmy ein und gab seiner Mama einen Kuss.

"Okay," agreed Jimmy, and he gave his mom a kiss.

Die Mama umarmte Jimmy und las ihren drei Kindern eine Gutenachtgeschichte vor. Während der Geschichte schliefen die Kinder ein.

Mom hugged Jimmy and read a bedtime story to her three children. During the story, the children fell asleep.

Mama gab ihnen allen einen Gutenachtkuss und ging in ihr eigenes Bett.

Mom gave all of them a goodnight kiss and went to sleep in her bed in her room.

Mitten in der Nacht wachte Jimmy auf.

In the middle of the night, Jimmy woke up.

Als er sah, dass Mama nicht bei ihm war, kletterte er aus dem Bett. Er nahm sein Kissen und seine Decke und schlich leise in Mamas und Papas Zimmer.

When he saw that Mom wasn't next to him, he got out of bed. He took his pillow and blanket, and sneaked quietly into Mom and Dad's room.

Dort schlüpfte er ins Bett, drückte Mama und schlief ein. So schliefen sie die ganze Nacht bis zum Morgen.

He got into their bed, hugged Mom, and fell asleep. They slept like that the whole night until the morning.

In der Nacht darauf erwachte Jimmy wieder, nahm seine Decke und sein Kissen und wollte wieder aus dem Zimmer schleichen, so wie die Nacht zuvor.

The next night, Jimmy woke up again, took his pillow and blanket, and tried to leave the room like the night before.

Doch da wachte sein mittlerer Bruder auf. „Jimmy, wohin gehst du?", fragte er.

But just then, his middle brother woke up. "Jimmy, where are you going?" he asked.

„Ähm, also…", stotterte Jimmy, „nirgendwohin. Geh wieder schlafen." Schnell rannte er in Mamas und Papas Zimmer. Jimmy schlich in ihr Bett und tat so, als würde er schlafen.

"Ah, ahh…," Jimmy stuttered, "nowhere. Go back to sleep." He quickly ran to his mom and dad's room. Jimmy sneaked into their bed and pretended to sleep.

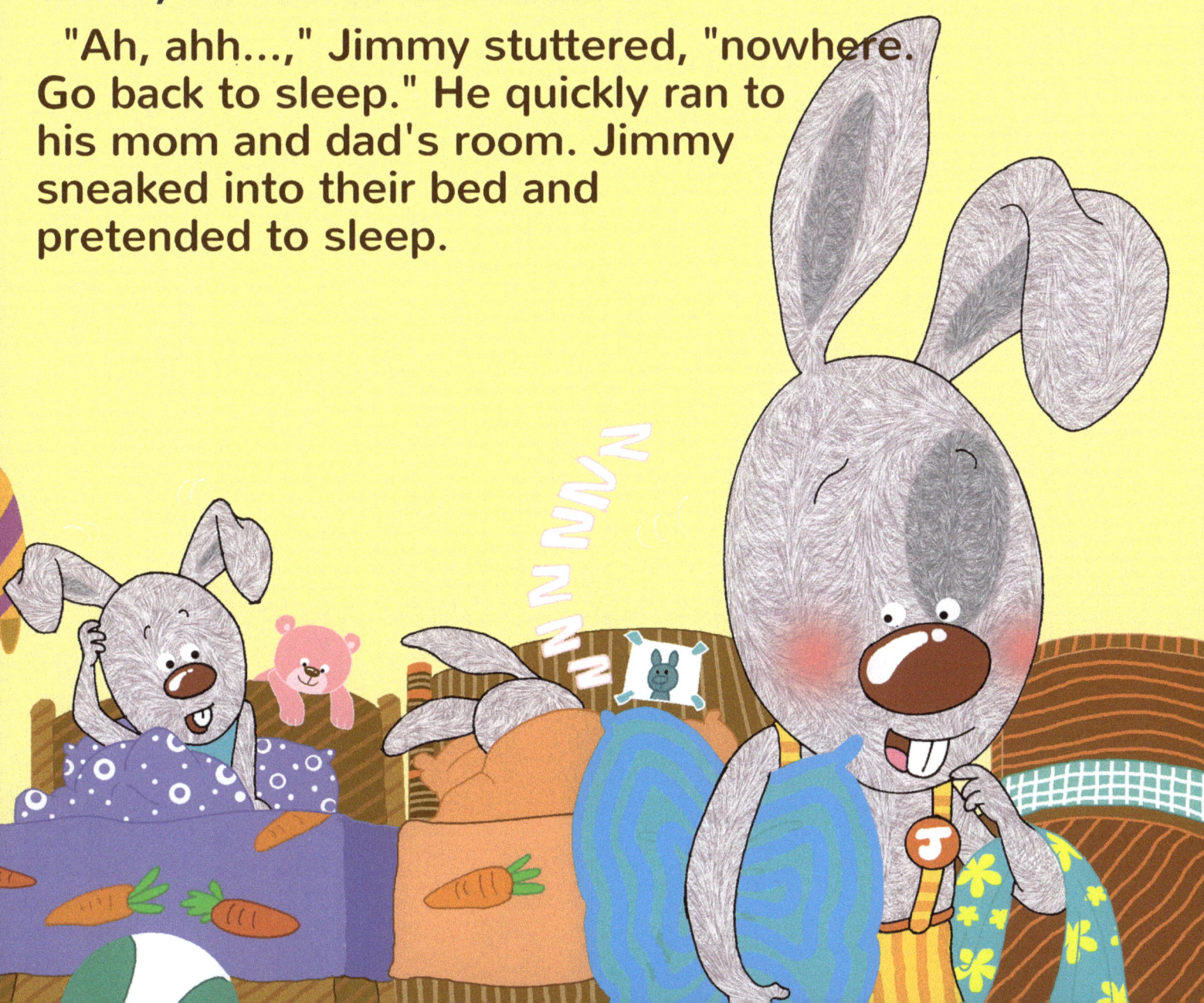

Doch sein mittlerer Bruder war hellwach. Ich frage mich, was hier los ist, dachte sein Bruder und beschloss, Jimmy zu folgen.

But his middle brother was wide awake. I wonder what's happening here, thought his brother and decided to follow Jimmy.

Als er entdeckte, dass Jimmy in Mamas und Papas Bett schlief, war er sehr verärgert.

When he discovered that Jimmy was sleeping in their mom and dad's bed, he was very upset.

So ist das also, dachte er. Wenn Jimmy das darf, dann will ich das auch!

So that's the way it is, is it? he thought. If Jimmy is allowed, then I want to also.

Und so kletterte er ebenfalls in das Bett ihrer Eltern.

With that, he got into their parents' bed as well!

Mama hörte die seltsamen Geräusche, öffnete die Augen und sah die beiden Kinder in ihrem Bett liegen.

Mom heard the strange noises, opened her eyes, and saw the two children in bed.

Sie machte Platz für die beiden und begnügte sich mit einer kleinen Ecke des Bettes.

She made room for them in the bed, by making do with a small corner of the bed for herself.

Und wieder schliefen sie so die ganze Nacht bis zum Morgen.

Again, they slept like that the whole night until the morning.

Das Gleiche passierte auch in der dritten Nacht. Jimmy erwachte, nahm sein Kissen und seine Decke und ging in das Zimmer seiner Eltern.

On the third night, the same thing happened. Jimmy woke up, took his pillow and blanket, and went to his parents' room.

Sein Bruder folgte ihm wieder und kroch auch mit seinem Kissen und seiner Decke in das Bett der Eltern.

His brother followed him again and got into their parents' bed together with his pillow and blanket.

Doch dieses Mal wachte auch der älteste Bruder auf.

But this time, the oldest brother also woke up.

Als der älteste Bruder seine beiden Geschwister bei Mama und Papa schlafen sah, wurde er sehr eifersüchtig.

When the oldest brother saw his two brothers sleeping together with Mom and Dad, he was very jealous.

Ich möchte auch in Mamas und Papas Bett schlafen, dachte er bei sich und sprang leise ins Bett.

I also want to sleep in Mom and Dad's bed, he thought and quietly jumped into the bed.

Mama und Papa konnten die ganze Nacht nicht schlafen. Sie wälzten sich hin und her und versuchten, ein wenig bequemer schlafen zu können.

Mom and Dad didn't rest the whole night. Tossing and turning, they tried to find the most comfortable way to sleep.

Für die kleinen Häschen war es aber auch nicht so einfach. Sie drehten sich im Bett hin und her und versuchten, es sich gemütlich zu machen, bis es fast Morgen war.

It wasn't easy for the little bunnies either. They turned over and over in the bed until it was almost morning.

Dann plötzlich...Bumm! ...Peng! ...brach das Bett zusammen!

Then suddenly...Boom! ...Bang! ...the bed broke!

„Was ist passiert?", rief Jimmy, als er aus dem Schlaf gerissen wurde.

"What happened?" Jimmy shouted as he woke up right away.

„Was machen wir denn jetzt?", fragte Mama traurig.

"What are we going to do now?" said Mom sadly.

„Wir werden ein neues Bett bauen müssen", antwortete Papa.

"We'll have to build a new bed," Dad announced.

Nach dem Frühstück ging die ganze Familie in den Wald, um ein neues Bett zu bauen.

After breakfast, the whole family went to the forest to build a new bed.

Nach einem langen arbeitsreichen Tag hatten sie ein großes, stabiles Bett aus Holz gebaut. Nun mussten sie es nur noch verzieren.

After a whole day's work, they had made a big, strong bed out of wood. The only thing left to do was decorate it.

„Wir haben beschlossen, unser Bett braun zu streichen", sagte Mama, „und ihr Kinder könnt euch aussuchen, mit welcher Farbe ihr eure Betten streichen möchtet."

"We've decided to paint our bed brown," said Mom, "and, you children, can repaint your beds whatever colors you like."

„Ich möchte Blau", sagte der älteste Bruder mit Begeisterung und rannte los, um sein Bett blau zu streichen.

"I want blue," said the oldest brother with excitement and ran to paint his bed blue.

„Und ich nehme die Farbe Grün", antwortete der mittlere Bruder glücklich.

"And I choose the color green," said the middle brother happily.

Jimmy nahm die Farbe Rot und die Farbe Gelb. Er mischte das Rot mit dem Gelb und machte daraus seine Lieblingsfarbe... **Orange!**

Jimmy took the color red and the color yellow. He mixed the red with the yellow and made his favorite color... **orange!**

Er strich sein Bett orange an und verzierte es mit roten und gelben Sternen.

He painted his bed orange and decorated it with red and yellow stars.

Nachdem er sein Bett fertig gestrichen hatte, rannte er zu Mama und rief stolz: „Mama, schau dir mein schönes Bett an! Ich liebe mein Bett so sehr."

After he finished, he ran to Mom and proudly shouted, "Mom, look at my beautiful bed! I love my bed so much."

Die Mama lächelte und umarmte Jimmy liebevoll. Seitdem hat Jimmy jede Nacht in seinem orangenen Bett geschlafen.

Mom smiled and gave Jimmy a big hug. Ever since then, Jimmy has slept in his orange bed every night.

Gute Nacht, Jimmy!
Goodnight, Jimmy!

www.ingramcontent.com/pod-product-compliance
Lightning Source LLC
LaVergne TN
LVHW072051060526
838200LV00061B/4712